Chewing Gum

A Sticky Treat

Elaine Landau

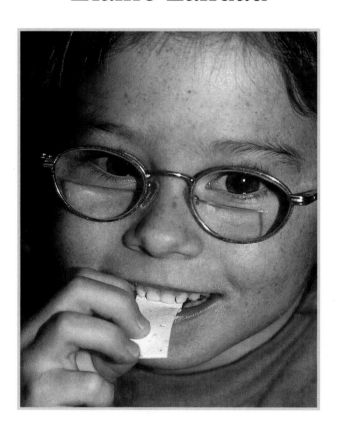

THE ROURKE PRESS, INC.

VERO BEACH, FLORIDA 32964

PHOTO CREDITS
Ben Klaffke

EDITORIAL SERVICES
Editorial Directions Inc.

Library of Congress Cataloging-in-Publication Data

Landau, Elaine.
    Chewing gum : a sticky treat / Elaine Landau.
        p. cm. — (Tasty treats)
    Includes bibliographical references.
    Summary: Briefly describes the origin of chewing gum, how it is made, ways it is enjoyed, and other interesting facts.
    ISBN 1-57103-335-1
    1. Chewing gum—Juvenile literature. [1. Chewing gum.] I. Title.

TX799 .L36 2000
641.3'38—dc21

                                                    00–022393

Printed in the USA

Contents

A Sticky Treat

Name a sticky taste treat with long-lasting flavor. One that feels smooth against your tongue. It comes in many shapes and colors. You chew but do not swallow it. Have you guessed the subject of this book? Get ready to read about chewing gum.

Gum comes in many different shapes and is fun to chew.

What Goes Into Gum

You can buy chewing gum in chunks, sticks, or balls. It comes in every color of the rainbow. But all chewing gum contains five things:

Gum base: The gum base holds the other ingredients together. It also makes chewing gum chewy. In the past, gum bases were usually made from **resins** and **latexes**. Resins are sticky materials from trees and plants. Latexes are milky fluids from plants. Today, there are newer gum base materials. These are made in factories. They allow the flavor to last even longer.

Sweeteners: Sugar and corn syrup make chewing gum sweet. Artifical sweeteners are used in sugar-free gum.

There are many different gum flavors.

Bubble gum is usually pink but can be other colors too.

Softeners: Vegetable oil products soften chewing gum. They make it moist and easy to chew.

Flavorings: Flavorings give chewing gum its taste. There are many different flavors. Adults tend to like **spearmint** and peppermint gum. Fruit flavors are popular among young people.

Colorings: Color adds to chewing gum's appeal. It makes you want to put it in your mouth. Some gums are known for their colors. Picture a piece of bubble gum. Did you think pink?

Bubble gum is fun!

From the Start...

People have chewed gumlike substances since early times. Scientists think cavepeople chewed a kind of gum. Later on, the women of ancient Greece used flavored gum daily.

Gum was chewed in ancient Greece. These Greek children still enjoy gum today.

The ancient Mayan Indians of Central America chewed gum. So did American Indian tribes in New England. These Indians used the gumlike resin from spruce trees. They taught the colonists to do the same.

By the late 1860s, modern chewing gum was invented. The gum was made from chicle. This is a gummy material from the sapodilla tree. Sapodilla trees grow in Central America's rainforests.

As time passed, gummakers improved their product. Soon chewing gum was as sought after as candy.

Gum is as popular as candy. It is displayed and sold with candy.

Sapodilla trees like this one provide the gummy material for chewing gum.

More Than a Sticky Treat

Is chewing gum good for your teeth? Surprisingly, the answer is yes. Chewing gum increases the **saliva** in your mouth. Saliva helps fight tooth decay. If you cannot brush after a snack, chewing gum helps.

There may be other benefits. Some studies show that chewing gum is relaxing. It also supposedly helps people stay alert. The army gives it to soldiers in combat zones. Astronauts chew it in their spacecrafts.

Chewing gum should never be used to replace brushing.

Some truck drivers say chewing gum keeps them alert.

Truck drivers on long **hauls** often use it. They claim chewing gum keeps them awake on the road.

Soldiers chew gum to relax.

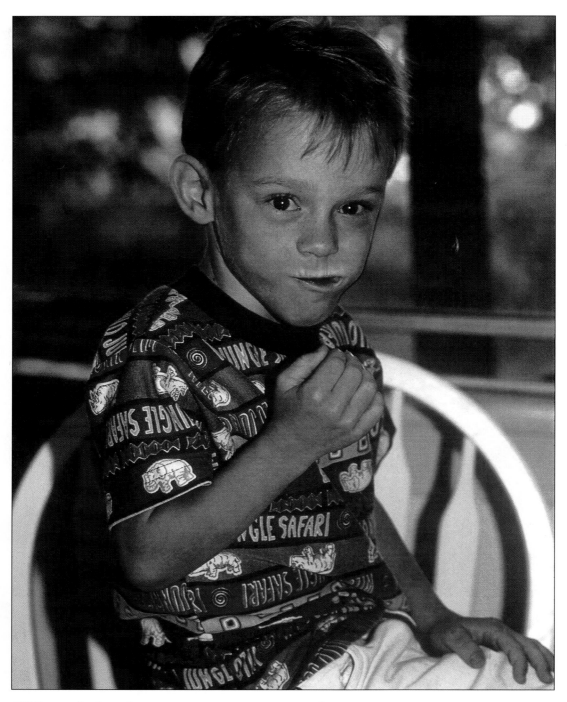

Kids and chewing gum seem to go together.
But adults actually chew more gum than children.

Interesting Chewing Gum
Fun Facts

 On the average, Americans chew more than 500 sticks of gum a year.

 More than 800 million a year is spent on chewing gum in the United States.

 Surprise! Adults chew far more gum than children.

 Swallowed gum does not stick to your intestines. It passes out of your system.

 During the 1920s, boxers chewed gum to strengthen their jaws. They hoped to be better able to take the punches.

Gum is chewed in countries around the world. You can choose from more than 150 chewing gum flavors in Japan. But more gum is still chewed in the United States than anywhere else!

There are many types of chewing gum.

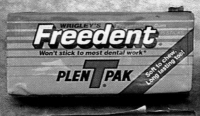

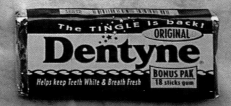

Glossary

haul (hawl) – to pull or bring something

latexes (LAY teksiz) – milky fluids taken from a plant

resins (REZ inz) – sticky materials taken from plants

saliva (suh LYE vuh) – a fluid given off by the glands in the cheeks and lower jaw

spearmint (SPEER mint) – an herb with a cool, minty flavor

For Further Reading

Hausherr, Rosemarie. *What Food Is This?* New York: Scholastic, 1994.

Landau, Elaine. *Sugar.* Danbury, Connecticut: Children's Press, 1999.

McGinty, Alice B. *Staying Healthy; Dental Care.* New York: Rosen, 1998.

Maynard, Christopher. *Why Are Pineapples Prickly? Questions Children Ask about Food.* New York: DK Publishing, 1997.

Index